EMILY SCALLY

This Book Belongs To

Before You Start Colouring

Welcome to a world of caring and kindness!

Inside you will find cute dogs and their animal friends alongside encouraging affirmations designed to brighten your day and calm your mind. Each page is a gentle invitation to slow down, be kind to yourself and connect with your creativity.

Use your favourite colouring pens or pencils and take your time. Before you begin colouring, don't forget to place a sheet of card behind the page to protect the next artwork. Every page is single-sided and has cut-out lines to follow on the back, so that you can remove it from the book and gift it to a loved one or display it as a kind reminder just for you.

You deserve kindness, especially from yourself!
You're safe here and you're doing great.

Have fun creating!

Test Colour Page

Celebrate yourself. Nobody knows what it takes to be you.

Someone feels better because you exist.

You're never a burden.
Please tell me everything.
I love listening to you ♡

You're doing what you can.
It is enough.
Self-hatred helps no one!

This morning I woke up and
I felt good because I have
you in my life ♡

Allow yourself to
feel your emotions.
Accept their existence.

Remember to rest and look after yourself. And don't forget that you are loved!!! ♡

I've gotta keep moving, even when I feel sad.

You are not an exception
in a world of lovable things.

Thank you for making my life better simply by being in it.
Thank you for being exactly who you are.

you deserve love.

Alternatives to 'I did nothing'
I rested.
I prioritised my needs.
I took a mental health day.
I gave myself what I needed.
I listened to my body.
I watched a movie or TV show that I love.
I allowed myself to recharge.

It's okay if you've changed and outgrown your old self. Whether that's mentally and/or physically, you have every right to live in whatever way makes you happy.

My nervous system doesn't have to live in the future. I can rest in the present moment. I'm allowed to be relaxed & happy.
SOAP

I want to keep going to see new versions of myself.

Some people will never be willing to take the time to listen and try to understand you. And it's not your fault or responsibility to teach them how!!

Sometimes doing the 'least'
is doing your most for the
day, and that's okay.

Trying just in case things get better.
There is no pride or glory in suffering. Take the time you need to feel better♡
You are never a burden and deserve to enjoy your life.

A special drink
makes life a little easier

It's okay if you're still healing from things from a long time ago.
Healing is hard and I'm proud of you.

Never give up!!
My wish for you is that you will fall in love with the world again.

Hold yourself with love through all seasons of your healing. You are lovable even when you aren't perfect.
i'm here for you.

Life can be really hard...
But there are a lot of good snacks.

Downtime is not
a waste of time.
Rest is essential.

BUG
One day you will wake up and breathe just like you used to. Without any heaviness.

Despite what you may think, you are not a burden, a failure, or whatever you call yourself. You belong on this earth as much as anyone else.

Keep going until you're glad that you did.

You can still make a beautiful life for yourself even if you feel like you've lost many years to grief or darkness or wounds that wouldn't close. You deserve to be happy.

My day is brighter
because of you.

I don't know what
the future has in store,
but I want to be with
you & figure it out together.

You are not hard
to love

Have faith in your journey
Everything had to happen exactly as it did...
...to get you to where you're going next.

To myself, I'm sorry for all the pain that you don't deserve.
Please go to bed knowing you are loved, valued and important.
You are worth fighting for. Please don't ever give up.

You're doing a really
good job & I'm sooOooo
proud of you!

The right people will make your heart feel seen and your nervous system feel calm.
They will make you feel brave enough & comfortable enough to not hide your emotions.

The fact that you're still here and still going means that you're a lot stronger than you give yourself credit for.

Your pace is the right pace for you. There is no deadline on healing or growth.
Keep going!
We got this!

i'm so glad I made it through the hard times so I could be alive to experience this...

I (really) love you. Please don't worry about tomorrow. Let's take a moment to relax & enjoy a little reward together. You deserve rest & support.

If all I do in this life is love you, that will be enough.
BUG GAMES
COLLECT HERE ↓

I'm so glad we found each other in this strange life.
BUG'S PIZZA
you rock!

You deserve a love that feels like safety. A love that chooses you on days where you don't feel your best. A love that reminds you : you are worthy, always.

About The Illustrator

EMILY SCALLY is a queer, autistic artist based in Hervey Bay. She began creating art as a form of therapy and now shares her work online as @artbylittlebug to inspire empathy and emotional honesty in others. Known for her bright, colourful style and characters often depicted crying, Emily aims to normalise sensitivity and self-compassion in a world that often tells people to 'toughen up'. Her art explores themes of kindness, validation and mental health, offering warmth and comfort to those who view it. A lifelong animal lover, especially of dogs, Emily creates with the hope of making others feel seen and understood.

@artbylittlebug

artbylittlebug.com

PENGUIN BOOKS

UK | USA | Canada | Ireland | Australia
India | New Zealand | South Africa | China

Penguin Books is part of the Penguin Random House group of companies
whose addresses can be found at global.penguinrandomhouse.com

First published by Penguin Books in 2026

Cover illustration by Emily Scally
Cover design by Adam Laszczuk © Penguin Random House Australia Pty Ltd
Illustrations by Emily Scally
Internal design by Adam Laszczuk

Printed and bound in Australia by Griffin Press, an accredited
ISO AS/NZS 14001 Environmental Management Systems printer

A catalogue record for this book is available from the National Library of Australia

ISBN 978 1 76162 099 7

penguin.com.au

We at Penguin Random House Australia acknowledge that Aboriginal and Torres Strait Islander peoples are the Traditional Custodians and the first storytellers of the lands on which we live and work. We honour Aboriginal and Torres Strait Islander peoples' continuous connection to Country, waters, skies and communities. We celebrate Aboriginal and Torres Strait Islander stories, traditions and living cultures; and we pay our respects to Elders past and present.